Why Single?

Why Single?

◆

"For the Glory of God"

Authored by: Clarence R. Hayes II

iUniverse, Inc.
New York Lincoln Shanghai

Why Single?
"For the Glory of God"

iUniverse, Inc.

For information address:
iUniverse, Inc.
2021 Pine Lake Road, Suite 100
Lincoln, NE 68512
www.iuniverse.com

ISBN: 0-595-31091-5

It is my belief that there is at least one book inside of everyone. The problem is how do we surface it to help ourselves and others. For me, it was failure—like being shipwrecked. I would rather be up the creek without a paddle, than in the creek without a boat. Hopefully, you get my point.

It is not very pleasant to try so many different strategies and yet unmistakenly come up with the same results…ANOTHER FAILED RELATIONSHIP. At this point I would like to mention some of the people who shaped some of my ideas, thoughts, and actions. They, that have helped, therefore, are in part responsible for the publication of this book.

Clarence R. Hayes Sr.—Father

Tiny Mae Hayes—Mother (deceased)

Hasene—Son

Brandi—Daughter

Mary Hayes-Leonard—Sister

All "my ladies", relatives, associates and enemies whom the good Lord has allowed to come into my life.

> St. Mark 12:29-31: And Jesus answered him, the first of all the command-ments is, Hear O Israel: The Lord our God is one Lord: and Thou shalt love the Lord thy God with all thy heart, and with all thy soul, and with all thy mind, and with all thy strength: this is the first commandment. And the sec-ond is like, namely this, Thou shalt love thy neighbor as thyself. There is none other commandment greater than these.

Contents

INTRODUCTION

On Tuesday, March 3, 1992, We started on this project called:

My goal is to finish this, my first book, as soon as possible for many reasons. First, I need to find out why I am single. Second, to determine why there are so many unhappy single people who would rather be married. Third, how to be happy in my situation and fourth, it has been my desire to write a book and until now the subject was not revealed.

I want to state that I am not now, or in the future, going to research this matter to gleam any ideas from others. My only source of wisdom will come from God the Father, God the Son—Jesus Christ, and God the Holy Spirit. My only interjections will be from my personal experiences, some acquired knowledge, and a lot of pain!

Therefore, I humbly start on this monumental task with the aid of my THREE HELPERS.

It is their inspiration which has given me this burning desire to try and answer some very pertinent questions that will aid a large growing segment of today's society—THE SINGLES!!!

What a privilege and honor to allow Their thoughts to flow through my mind in order to share this book with you.

We hope that you will be open minded enough to receive these reasons, suggestions, and possibly conclusions. It is our desire that you gain victory as well as understanding about your singlehood and the singleness of your friends.

The methods employed will be in the form of questions and, yes, answers from the living Word of God. To reiterate, my only reference book will be The Holy Bible—the infallible Word of God.

We anticipate your acceptance of God's Word, my theories, and some conclusions. It will be your choice. So be patient and hang in there with an open mind until you have read the final word. You'll see, therefore, how dependent I am and will be upon my Helpers.

> Psalms 121:1-2: I will lift up mine eyes unto the hills from whence cometh my help. My help cometh from the Lord which made heaven and earth.

My limited life experiences, and God-given common sense will also help lay the foundation. I can only give out what has been given to me. My knowledge is limited so, therefore, I will solicit some comments from those who may or may not be an authority on this subject matter.

You may have already formulated your own conclusions about singlehood. But, before you close the doors of your mind, you have got to read this book.

So, if you are ready, then We are ready to begin.

> St. John 8:32: And ye shall know the truth and the truth shall make you free.

PREFACE

Now this is what I would like for you to do. This little exercise of your mind will, without a doubt, start you on the road to discovery, recovery, victory and, most importantly, understanding.

Remember the times when you were asked the who, why, when, what, how, and where questions about any given subject matter? Yes, you got it—that's the game we are about to play.

To start the game, THINK-PONDER-MEDITATE and—WONDER on these questions:

WHO————————— CREATED THE GAP?
WHY————————— CAN'T WE GET ALONG?
WHEN———————— DO WE LET GO?
WHAT———————— IS THE REAL—FOR REAL—PROBLEM?
DO YOU KNOW———— WHAT LOVE IS?
HOW————————— CAN I RECONSTRUCT MY LIFE?
WHERE——————— IS MY MATE?

This book unfortunately will not be a quick, fix-it right now, publication. Yet it can be. One can never underestimate the power of the living Word of God.

> Hebrews 4:12: For the word of God is quick and powerful and sharper than any two-edged sword piercing even to the dividing asunder of the soul and spirit, and of the joints and marrow and is a discerner of the thoughts and intents of the heart.

Even if you're not a believer, I challenge you to stop right now and ask God to give to you "THE SPIRIT OF WISDOM AND REVELATION IN THE KNOWLEDGE OF HIM." This will help you understand His love for you, and give you faith to believe in HIM. The result will be forgiveness of any and all sins plus the promised abundant life.

Those very simple requests are the tools you will need to fulfill your life's every need. One more additional request that will be very helpful would be to ask God to help you understand and really get to know and appreciate who you are.

Philippians 1:6: Being confident of this very thing, that he which hath begun a good work in you will perform it until the day of Jesus Christ:

Now back to those questions! Have you come up with any answers yet? Well we may have a few for you—the longer you stick with Us. Accurate answers bring forth knowledge that helps you gain victory over ignorance. Truth will solidify your interpersonal relationships. You may have already gained the victory, but hopefully it was not at someone else's physical or mental loss.

Proverbs 2:10-11: When wisdom entereth into thine heart, and knowledge is pleasant unto thy soul; discretion shall preserve thee, understanding shall keep thee.

Can your life get any better? Can your love life flourish into a beautiful floral arrangement? Are you willing to love someone for who they are? Do you love yourself for who you are? Are you really happy? Are you depending on someone else to make you happy? Am I truly with the person I want or need?

Amos 3:3: Can two walk together; except they be agreed?

There are a lot of questions that need correct and unbiased answers. A lot of people can give you an answer but, is it the correct answer?

Remember some of those tests that were taken in school? Just because you filled in the space, it didn't necessarily mean you gave the correct answer. One can liken this to some of the advice we have given or that has been given to us.

Proverbs 30:5-6: Every word of God is pure: He is a shield unto them that put their trust in him. Add thou not unto his words, lest he reprove thee, and thou be found a liar.

WHO—CREATED THE GAP??

First, we might not believe a GAP exists between males and females, but unfortunately one does. Secondly, WE MUST BE WILLING TO DO SOMETHING ABOUT IT!!

We are all products of our past and present environments, relationships, and role models we have chosen to emulate either consciously or subconsciously. All the aforementioned experiences have been stored in our own PC—personal computer—called the human brain.

The human brain has an enormous storage capacity. Its instantaneous recall capability focuses most often on negative aspects especially when we have been offended. It is a small wonder why we act the way we do.

In this instant informational age, we are often force-fed sensationalized negativism by the media, periodicals and our own vivid imaginations. Now you can clearly see why we act and react as we do towards our mates. Haven't you ever wondered why, or questioned WHO is the root cause of these mental dilemmas? Does this sound like the reaction of a sound mind dealing with disappointments? Am I normal? What have I done this time? What have you done? It's your fault! I don't need this so, GOOD BYE!!

It is no wonder that we are emotionally distraught, and overwhelmed with anger and bitterness. Filled with resentment and frustration, the last thing we want to hear about is another failed relationship. We then, have the tendency to quickly take gender sides, without knowing all the facts. Suddenly, the problems become too big to handle without an unhealthy confrontation. Sad to say, we now have added more garbage into our PC, and the GAP widens.

> II Timothy 1:7: For God hath not given us the spirit of fear; but of power, and of love, and of a sound mind.

We tend to take our frustration out on the ones we love, or anyone else who will listen to our tirades.

Meanwhile, WHO (Satan) is somewhere else plotting his next move to create additional havoc between men and women. Question. Why would you want to get into a relationship if you aren't willing to focus on love, joy, peace, and happiness? Don't we spend too much time focusing on what WHO is doing to our affairs, instead of kicking him out?

Almighty God did not create us to constantly be at each other's nerve centers. We were created to be fruitful, to multiply and to have dominion over the earth.

Let's look at God's word and his creation of mankind.

> Genesis 1:27, 28: So God created man in his own image, in the image of God created he him; male and female created he them. And God blessed them, And God said unto them, Be fruitful, and multiply, and replenish the earth, and subdue it: and have dominion over the fish of the sea, and over the fowl of the air, and over every living thing that moveth upon the earth.

Let's look at how God made provision for man. He gave man this commandment:

> Genesis 2:15-17: And the Lord God took the man, and put him into the garden of Eden to dress it and keep it. And the Lord God commanded the man, saying, Of every tree of the garden thou mayest freely eat: But of the tree of the knowledge of good and evil, thou shalt not eat: for in the day that thou eatest thereof thou shalt surely die.

Next, God gave man what he needed to complete him—A WOMAN!!

> Genesis 2:18, 21-25: And the Lord God said, It is not good that the man should be alone; I will make him a help meet for him. And the Lord God caused a deep sleep to fall upon Adam, and he slept: and he took one of his ribs, and closed up the flesh instead thereof: And the rib, which the Lord God had taken from man, made he woman, and brought her unto the man. And Adam said, This is now bone of my bone, flesh of my flesh: she shall be called Woman, because she was taken out of Man. Therefore shall a man leave his father and his mother, and shall cleave unto his wife; and they shall be one flesh. And they were both naked, the man and his wife, and were not ashamed.

I would like to point something out to you for your understanding. Up to this point there was no problem or GAP between us. All of man's necessities were met by God. Then something happened that caused the big problem. WHO made his appearance and the GAP was created. Before I go on, I would like to make this one profound conclusion based on the above facts of God's creation and His provisions for mankind: "We can now stop blaming God when our relationships hit rock bottom."

Our problems started with WHO!

> Genesis 3:1-5: Now the serpent was more subtle than any beast of the field which the Lord God had made. And he said unto the woman, Yea, hath God said, Ye shall not eat of every tree of the garden? And the woman said unto the serpent, We may eat of the fruit of the trees of the garden: But of the fruit of the tree which is in the midst of the garden, God hath said, Ye shall not eat of it, neither shall ye touch it, lest ye die. And the serpent said unto the woman, Ye shall not surely die: For God doth know that in the day ye eat thereof, then your eyes shall be opened, and ye shall be as gods, knowing good and evil.

That's right WHO caused the original split between man, woman, mankind and God. Stop now and read the entire third chapter of Genesis. In verses 12-13 you will see man and woman putting the blame on someone else, rather than themselves. Likewise, today we usually blame someone else. We need to get to the cancerous core of our problemed relationships to defeat WHO and stop the widening of the GAP.

See basically it is our disobedience and our rebellious nature that allows WHO to step between us and our happiness. We need to quit pointing our fingers at our present and former mates. Realize this, the serpent did not start out being our friend. He is not our friend now. Satan or WHO comes in our lives for one purpose only:

> St. John 10:10: The thief cometh not, but for to steal, and to kill, and to destroy; I am come that they might have life, and that they might have it more abundantly.

Wow! You might be asking, how does all this fit into my present or past situations. It fits in everywhere and in every way! Therefore, you must be patient enough to hang with me. Your particular circumstance might not be covered. But there will be enough similarities and principles that will enable you to finish this book and be HEALED, DELIVERED, AND SET FREE! All it will take is BELIEF and your ACTION upon what you believe.

It is important that you understand why we sometimes think and act the way we do. WHO has power to motivate our thought patterns IF we let him.

WHO is the force and source behind our being force-fed negativism and sensationalism. When was the last time you have read or heard about couples that are getting along, building strong families and sharing the abundant life Christ speaks about in the above verse.

Everyday we are bombarded by the negatives. It is no wonder we think and act the way we do. Have you noticed that I haven't mentioned the use of the telephone yet! We need our minds cleansed and renewed by putting in the Good News. Certainly there must be at least one relationship from which we can glean some positive input in this world.

God has equipped every man and woman with a conscience and has written His laws on the fleshly tables of their heart. In spite of the wiles of the devil, the Lord God has made provisions for us to succeed in our interpersonal relationships IF we are willing to do it His way!

> II Corinthians 3:3: Forasmuch as ye are manifestly declared to be epistles of Christ ministered by us, written not with ink, but with the Spirit of the living God; not in tables of stone, but in fleshly tables of the heart.

We are now without excuse! Yes, most if not all of our problems were caused by the suggestions of WHO. Why do we always have to act upon his suggestions? No, we don't, not any more. With God's help, we can change the way we handle ourselves with our loved ones. Most of us know the difference between right and wrong. We know when we blame or put down others for their shortcomings, it will take the spotlight off of us momentarily. Accept this as a fact, it could be you causing the Gap.

Disobedience and ungodly actions come after someone thinks to do them!

Now we know WHO motivates these acts, but, we are the ones who carry them out. Remember, the time when you tried to get even with your mate. Particularly the time and effort you took to plot your revenge. These acts most often cause guilt, plus other emotional problems and the Gap widens even more. We all need help in this area—and we need it NOW!

One subtle approach Satan uses is curiosity. He used it on Eve and he is still using it today. Often you have heard that "curiosity killed the cat." I didn't coin that statement, and you might be wondering why it is mentioned now? Well, let's create this curiosity for instance. You and your mate are having the most stupendous relationship. All of a sudden someone's mind starts to wander to another party. Their mind gets the best of them and they seek out new ground. You are now left with hurt feelings. See mankind is always looking to please his flesh and you know WHO knows this. It is easy to see how temptations are placed in our lives. WHO IS FOREVER ENTICING US TO DO HIS WILL! Whosoever, and whensoever we listen and do what WHO tells us to do, we are headed for a disastrous outcome. You will pay an even bigger consequence.

> Romans 6:23: For the wages of sin is death; but the gift of God is eternal life through Jesus Christ our Lord.

We will often wind up socially busted and emotionally wrecked. Some even become unwed mothers or guilt-ridden from an abortion. Not to mention venereal diseases. Those are but a few consequential examples of the ones who listen and do what WHO bids them to do. The Gap continues to widen. HOWEVER THERE IS HOPE AND IT IS THROUGH HAVING A RIGHT RELATIONSHIP WITH JESUS CHRIST!

This last paragraph will cover some of the problems that often occur in our relationships masterminded by WHO. OVERCOMING THE WORLD AND IT'S EVER CHANGING VALUE SYSTEM. Gone are the days of courtships—THE OLD FASHION WAY. Respect, chastity, hand-holding, and abstinence were the thoughts and practices of yesterday. This present day puts more pressure on having a sexual encounter rather than knowing someone's last name. You are not readily or socially accepted unless you have had sex. The god of this world promotes us to have sex, sex, sex! In all actuality all he wants us to do is sin, sin, sin! That is only a small part—wait until you see the big picture!

> I John 2:15-16: Love not the world, neither the things that are in the world. If any man love the world, the love of the Father is not in him. For all that is in the world, the lust of the flesh, and the lust of the eyes, and the pride of life is not of the Father, but is of the world.

This section was not written to glorify WHO, but only to help establish a foundation. Also to get you focused on WHO the real, for real, enemy of mankind is. WHO is, and has been a liar, thief, murderer, and has ruined countless of millions of lives. Only through JESUS can we stop this trend in our lives.

> Joshua 4:24: That all the people of the earth might know the hand of the Lord, that it is mighty: that ye might fear the Lord your God forever.

Remember my THREE HELPERS. They were, and are now still my solution. They are helping me to share this book with you. They are more than willing and able to help you out of all your dilemmas. I don't know about you but, I would like to have a meaningful, and worthwhile Christ honoring relationship NOW!

> Genesis 18:14: Is any thing too hard for the Lord? At the time appointed I will return unto thee, according to the time of life, and Sarah shall have a son.

God provided man with what he needed for physical completion. That was, and still is, A WOMAN. Not several at one time, but ONE. Same goes for women, pairs not spares. I don't know if I told you, but that was one of my problems. Of course you know by now WHO suggested the spares!! I listened and I paid the big price—TWO MARRIAGES—TWO CHILDREN—TWO DIVORCES!!! I can't speak for all humanity, and I certainly haven't experienced everything, but what I have told you is the truth. REMEMBER "WHO" IS THE ENEMY NOT YOUR MATE!

> Ecclesiastes 2:24-26: There is nothing better for a man, than that he should eat and drink, and that he should make his soul enjoy good in his labor. This also I saw, that it was from the hand of God. For who can eat, or who else can hasten hereunto, more than I? For God gives to a man that is good in his sight wisdom, and knowledge, and joy: but to the sinner he gives travail, to gather and to heap up, that he may give to him that is good before God. This also is vanity and vexation of spirit.

I would just like to touch on the ally WHO uses to carry out his bidding. The ally's name is: THE FLESH. If you lift your right arm and place it before your eyes, you would see a member of your flesh. I wanted to make sure you know without a doubt what flesh is. Another point we need to insert is: YOU CAN NEVER TRUST YOUR FLESH OR ANY ONE ELSES. As you continue on this journey, you will see more acts of the flesh. Just remember this. WHO AND YOUR FLESH WILL DESTROY YOU, AND THAT MY FRIEND IS THE TRUTH THAT YOU SHOULD KNOW NOW!!!

> Romans 8:1: There is therefore now no condemnation to them which are in Christ Jesus, who walk not after the flesh, but after the spirit.

WHY—CAN'T WE GET ALONG?

Well, that's a loaded question if there ever was one. Some people will say that bad times usually last longer than good times. Even if you don't agree, most often we focus on the negatives rather than on the positive. When the bad times occur in our lives and we stay focused on them, this causes gaps which end in split ups.

Split-ups are never without pain and emotional unrest. Most often these indifferences are the tests of wills that are motivated by pride. Pride coupled with winning by any means and at any cost is called SELFISHNESS. Before split-ups occur, matters usually go unsettled. It's like all the present day wars that are going on throughout this world. In order to reach an agreement that's satisfactory to both parties, terms and conditions must be met. Agreeable peaceful solutions should be the goal. The common enemy to this ideal solution is PRIDE.

> Proverbs 29:23: A man's pride shall bring him low: but honor shall uphold the humble in spirit.

Pride caused my first marriage to end in divorce. Many times I have wanted to kick myself in my PRIDE!! Decisions had to be made as whether or not it is worth staying together. Each situation is different. But if it's your pride that is foremost in this decision, then I say "stick and stay." The grass is not that green on the other side. If there are children as a result of your union, then that's an additional reason to stay.

The natural need to insure or gain victory, in any given situation is to preserve SELF at any and all cost. Self is seated #1 with the highest priority to preserve it, so that it can survive yet another day. Guess what? In some circumstances you had better think that way. But, on the other hand aren't we a little too selfish at times? Does the world truly revolve around me? Do I have to have my way all the time?

Doesn't what other people or my mate think or say have any merit? Isn't it time for me to grow up and realize that there are over 5 billion people on this earth and, they have opinions too. This may be a little hard for some of you, but others will hear what God has to say when we get too selfish.

> II Peter 2:10: But chiefly them that walk after the flesh in the lust of unclean-ness, and despise government. Presumptuous are they self-willed, they are not afraid to speak evil of dignities.

Look, I was a very very selfish man at one time. Only with the help of ALMIGHTY God am I a little better now. See I ask God through Jesus Christ to show me my weaknesses, my shortcomings, and my selfish ways. I didn't like what I saw. Now I realize why I had so many disasters. It was always easy for me to blame others. Even after learning about WHO, I would still have an excuse or reason to shift the blame on others. That's our nature. After my pity party was over, I would look for comfort in the next relationship. Armed with pain, unfor-giveness, and revenge, I would try again. Whenever you go into a new relation-ship with unsettled differences from the last, you will be in a bigger mess than before.

My problems started early in life. When I was 14 years old, my first puppy love affair went sour. She broke my little heart. I didn't know how to let go of the hurt feelings at that time in my life. Lady #1 had the nerve to dump me for some-one else. I went home, I'm proud to say and cried. Also at fourteen, boys usually resent their mothers telling them anything to do with which they disagree. My loving mother never bit her tongue when it came to raising me. I thank the good Lord that she didn't. And there was always my daddy there to maintain respect and order in the house with love and the rod when necessary.

The only way I knew to channel my pain and frustrations was to hurt others before they hurt me. Unfortunately most people selfishly think that way also. I'm not saying that we consciously think that way. But who really knows what we have buried subconsciously. Look, we live in a "me first" society and that's the rule of thumb. All I can do now, privately and publicly, is to say "I AM SIN-CERELY SORRY AND WILL YOU FORGIVE ME?"

While I am on the subconscious, one does not realize how much unforgive-ness we have stored there. Many books have been written on the power of the subconscious mind. After reading a few of them, I can stand on my past state-ments concerning our negative thought patterns. The more garbage we have stored in our subconscious mind, the more quickly we get angry and seek revenge. We sometimes act out our past anger on our present mates—which is totally unfair. This act plants seeds of failure. Let me ask you something, "can you honestly learn to love and respect someone who still holds on to anger and unforgiveness?"

Ephesians 4:26: Be ye angry, and sin not: let not the sun go down upon your wrath:

You can protect self and learn to respect others through FORGIVENESS. You will not be compromising your pride or self worth by admitting that on some occasions you could have been wrong. On the other hand, by saying the hardest two words in our language," I'M SORRY," you will become a bigger and better person, even if you think you are right. Deep down, the other person just might know, that they are the one who is wrong.

This next portion is very touchy, but it needs to be said anyway. A growing segment of today's society has an identity problem. I have met and talked with many people down through the years who have lost out on love affairs. They lost out on love to someone of the same sex. They found out their partner went both ways. Yes, that is one big reason WHY!!

God's words speak a lot louder than mine ever will concerning this sin. This is also one of WHO'S tricks whether you admit it or not. The BIBLE is full of what God thinks about this. Read if you may Romans 1:16-32. There are some very bitter people who simply won't or don't trust anymore. Not everyone accepts this lifestyle. I once dated a very beautiful swinger, who I would never imagined was into this type of behavior. Boy, did I get the shock of my life. After that, every lady was placed under the big microscope.

This condition is running rampant in America today. People are confused and devastated by the actions of others. This is a sin problem, not a lifestyle, and it needs to be dealt with like all sin that was created by WHO. That's the last thing one should have to worry about when a relationship is developing.

Romans 1:26-27: For this cause God gave them up unto vile affections; for even their women did change the natural use into that which is against nature; And likewise also the men, leaving the natural use of the woman, burned in their lust one toward another; men with men working that which is unseemly, and receiving in themselves that recompense of their error which is meet.

Now if you have been lured into this trap, ask God to get you out NOW! God can forgive you and turn you into the man or woman he created you to be. God didn't make a mistake. Okay, I have heard people say, "that's the way I was born." Don't fall for that, it's a learned behavior pattern. That's why we all need to be BORN AGAIN. Let the cleansing blood of Jesus Christ wash you as white as snow.

Most people have heard the biblical account of Sodom and Gomorrah. Am I correct? Did you know that God asked them to repent and they didn't, therefore they were destroyed? Read Isaiah 1:10-31 with emphasis on verses 18-20.

> Isaiah 1:18-20: Come now, and let us reason together, smith the Lord: though your sins be as scarlet, they shall be as white as snow; though they be like crimson, they shall be as wool. If ye be willing and obedient, ye shall eat good of the land: But if ye refuse and rebel, ye shall be devoured with the sword: for the mouth of the Lord hath spoken it.

See God is merciful and willing to forgive. You see my friend unnatural relationships causes gaps of mistrust and disrespect. We will definitely be covering the latter in the next paragraph.

DISRESPECT

Many folks have lost their lives because of those ten letters. WHY? Disrespect is the opposite of respect. Back in the seventies, a very famous recording artist recorded a record entitled RESPECT. Everybody should want respect and know how to respect others. That's the golden rule. Quit giving your relationship the kiss of death by your disrespect of others. When you plant seeds of disrespect, they come back at you somewhere down the line. What goes around, comes around.

> St. Matthew 7:12: Therefore all things whatsoever ye would that men should do to you, do ye so to them: for this is the law and the prophets.

Just to illustrate this disrespect a little. Remember those harsh words you gave out when you lost control. Remember when you provoked an argument because you had a chip on your shoulder. Remember when you falsely accused your friend. Remember when you laid your hands on them because you were mad. Those are but a few reasons for you to think about.

Men, we must realize that we can't out talk or out argue a woman. Women are very good at this. When we lose, it frustrates our egos to the point of severe anger which has lead some to violence in the past. I believe that we as men must establish the attitude of respect by love. We must be creative enough to secure this as a foundation from jump street. Talk about these things first, to see if respect is high on her priority list. You need to know this right away. If you can't use respect as one of the foundations to build upon, then there will be no real love for each other.

> Proverbs 15:18: A wrathful man stirreth up strife: but he that is slow to anger appeaseth strife.

Women, on the other hand, respect should be more important than how much money he makes. Abuse, whether physical or mental, should never be tolerated. I know many women that are in abusive situations because of money. Remember, when and if, you survive a situation like this, you will take that baggage into the next relationship. Stop abuse before it starts. I have dated a number of ladies that have said from day one that they "didn't play that hitting stuff," and I believed them.

Proverbs 21:23: Whoso keepeth his mouth and his tongue, keepeth his soul from troubles.

Proverbs 6:23-24: For the commandment is a lamp; and the law is light; and reproofs of instruction are a way of life: to keep thee from the evil woman, from the flattery of the tongue of a strange woman.

When you have a destructive type of attitude, and have your defense mechanism set in place, you are not ready for love. You are prepared for war. Well just suppose your next is in the same boat as you are in. This is a very potentially volatile situation. It looks more like a couple of warriors preparing for battle, instead of a romance.

Without God's peace you would have two time bombs waiting to explode. That is a very serious way to start a friendship also very unhealthy. The unfortunate thing is that many relationships start this way. After the initial formalities are gotten out of the way and the sex is incorporated into this union, then the fuse is lit. Here comes #1 SELF.

St. John 14:27: Peace I leave with you, my peace I give unto you not as the world, give I unto you. Let not your heart be troubled neither let be afraid.

Most of our selfishness is centered around three little words. Although they are somewhat similar in meaning, they are definitely different in scope. Well if you haven't guessed them by now, they are NEEDS, WANTS, and DESIRES. We will try at best to break them down so that you will be able to see how you may have fared in your interpersonal relationship with others.

NEED:

Need is lack of a useful or desired thing; necessity; a requirement. Life would be extremely difficult without our basic needs being met. When you look at the word need, and put it into it's proper context within the structure of our lives, we will see it boils down to FOOD, CLOTHING, SHELTER, WATER, and PURPOSE IN LIFE. Those are the basic survival needs for mankind.

Philippians 4:19: But my God shall all your need according to his riches in glory by Christ Jesus.

WANTS:

Wants means wished for; wishes; lacks; desires or craves. In the above meanings, as you can clearly see, wants are not always necessary. Don't get me wrong, wants are necessary and they should be met, providing you put your need or needs first!

Psalm 23:1: The Lord is my shepherd; I shall not want.

DESIRES:

Desires are wished for: asked for; longing, yearning.

Now the priority list should be in its proper sequence. Desires should not take precedence over needs and wants in your life. Also when you look at wants and desires, the meanings have more similarity than needs.

Psalm 37:4: Delight thyself also in the Lord; and he shall give thee the desires of thine heart.

When you carefully analyze those meanings, and the attached Word of God, you just might see a different way to handle people in the near future. One might say, "Does God really care about my needs, wants, and desires?" Yes, God does. In Philippians 4:19, you will find an often quoted passage of scripture, but did you know that is also one of God's promises. To truly shed some light on that promise, this word processing machine that I am using right now was supplied to me by God. He knew that I had genuine NEED of one to continue the project we started last March!!!!!!!!!!!! TO GOD BE THE GLORY!!!!!!!!!!!!!!

To further illustrate my point, I have found out that my want of a Virtuous Woman found in Proverbs 31, and desire of a new 760 Volvo will be met as they move up into the need column. Speaking of that Volvo, my son Hasene promised to turn pro and win The Volvo International Tennis Tournament and give it to me. Hurry my son hurry!!

Psalm 27:14: Wait on the Lord: be of good courage, and he shall strengthen thine heart: wait I, say on the Lord.

God is omniscient and will keep His word. You need to get to know Him. God also knows what is best for us, and what is most needful. He also knows the time in which you/we can handle them. Most of us entertain selfish and useless thoughts in our wants and desire areas. Those thoughts, and I need to be very careful at this point, are not to be confused with your DREAMS. So go with me and try to separate DREAMS from wants and desires. For instance, a twelve year old boy DREAMS that one day he would drive in the INDY 500. He really WANTS this now. His overwhelming DESIRE is to cross the finish line first after seeing the checkered flag. All of those thoughts are perfectly normal, but who would give him the millions of dollars needed to participate in the race at twelve years old.

I didn't mean to dwell on those issues that long, but my HELPERS deemed them too important to let them be scarcely mentioned. As we continue to move through this section on WHY we can't get along, I need to mention the word EGO. When you group EGO with PRIDE and SELFISHNESS, you can readily see that we could close out this section now, and let you fill in the blank pages.

> Isaiah 55:8: For my thoughts are not your thoughts, neither are your ways my ways, saith the Lord.

Egos—whether they are healthy or unhealthy—are very difficult to let go of. I am not sure we will ever let go of our egos, or if we are supposed to in the first place. But there is one thing that I do know—our egos are not supposed to be offensive, abusive, intolerable, insensitive or just plain nasty to other people. It shouldn't matter even if we have been the offended party.

You should never stay in an abusive, demoralizing or inhumane relationship. There are far too many of those types going on and have been going on for years. Most of those types end violently anyway. The problem is, that most of us know of at least one of these exist within our families, friends, or people we associate with.

As we are updated of those current events, we formulate opinions and the GAP widens even more. We often vent our frustrations out on our mates. Leave the boxing to those who are getting paid to do so.

It boils down to the fact that we have simply lost RESPECT for one another for multiple of reasons. Some were mentioned before and others will be addressed as we journey on. Whatever the reasons, they are locked within our PC, with our hands on the recall button. Hit that button now and ask God to show you what it is, so that you and He can do something about it.

Saint Matthew 7:7: Ask, and it shall be given you; seek and ye shall find; knock and it shall be opened unto you:

Was the GAP caused by rejection, incest, a dominate parent, broken-hearted relationships, other people's problems, media bombardments, or what? If you are still having trouble ask God, in Jesus name, to show you what it is. It's that important. Don't you want to have the best for yourself? Well so does God—whether you believe me or not. When your toaster breaks you do not usually go to the auto mechanic do you? So go back to the maker of us, THE CREATOR. By the way he is not at the zoo!!!

St. John 14:13, 14: And whatsoever ye shall ask in my name, that will I do that the Father may be glorified in the Son. If ye shall ask anything in my name, I will do it.

Of course there are many other reasons WHY we can't get along. Likewise there are many reasons why we can get along, IF WE WANT TO. Sometimes we simply are with the wrong person—INCOMPATIBILITY. There are some people who are just not the one. You can not put a round peg into a square hole. Admit to each other that you both have erred in judgement and move on. Hopefully, you haven't severely injured someone's feelings or egos. But that's another problem. It shouldn't take years to find this out. We should be patient enough to find out if we have things in common. Compatibility will usually surface pretty quickly, if you to have been honest with each other. I haven't mentioned that friends stick when lovers don't. That's going to be covered later, I promise.

Somehow we must gain victory over self, and realize that there is another human being involved whom God also loves and for whom Jesus Christ died. Now you might see that someone else is important in the mix of things. Their thoughts, opinions, concerns and needs should be met and they also are important.

Spend quality time talking. Get to know them. Find out what they want, what they are thinking about and where they are going in life. Determine quickly whether you are willing to help them. Find out if you are compatible with them. Learn to put them first so they will learn to put you first!

St. Matthew 16:24: Then Jesus said unto his disciples, If any man will come after me, let him deny himself, and take up his cross, and follow me.

We all need a lot of work to remove the ISH out of selfish and the DIS out of disrespect. And somehow put those two words together and come up with SELF-RESPECT.

Allow that to be your badge of honor and you will be surprised how you will treat others and how others will treat you. Suddenly, we will be able to overcome this character flaw and start to get along.

I know this principle goes against our human nature. Is human nature working now or did it work in the past? Somewhere down this pathway we must be willing to change in order to succeed. I'll give you an example of what I mean. I want you to do this exercise with me. I am going to type some words and what I want you to do is put SELF in front of these words: centerness—righteous—seeking—gratification—willed—reliant—indulgent—a wareness. Would you like to become involved with someone who possessed these character traits?

Hopefully you have gotten my point about WHY we can't get along! Believe me I'm not saying that you are not to protect yourself. Remove yourself from unhealthy relationships. Never let your flesh keep or dictate to you your desire to stay. Our selfishness is usually centered on these three words with similar meanings but diverse in realities—NEEDS; WANTS; DESIRES.

WHEN—DO WE LET GO?

Let go of what?!!!. Well, for one thing PAST FAILED RELATIONSHIPS. Before going on, let me share this with you. "All failures are not necessarily bad." They can be valuable learning experiences. It would depend solely upon the viewpoint one would take. We often here of "the lemon to lemonade" axiom quoted often today. Lemonade is one of my favorite year-round refreshing drinks. Therefore you need lemons in order to make lemonade. We need failures to know what success is.

Now I know, you have heard and probably used this often quoted statement. "I will forgive you, BUT I won't forget it." If you have held to that principle, then today, right now in fact, LET IT GO. Holding on to not forgetting is counter productive and will destroy your now and future. How do you press the erase buttom of your mind? Some people would tell you it's impossible. Well it AIN'T!

> Luke 18:27: And he said, the things which are impossible with men are possible with God.

I could end there, but there is much more my Helpers want to share with you concerning this principle. One of the opening scriptures we used, was "knowing the truth." Many people do not know the truth and they will give you incorrect advice, that we readily accept. I for one lived by this rule. "Now I might forgive you, BUT I will never ever forget it." My question is, "do you live by this same rule, also?"

Adhering to just the forgiving part "with certain conditions" does not cut the mustard. I still had the "not forgetting" part locked in my heart. Which also meant that I had the key to open the door to rehash the past whenever there was need too. That's why we have to let it go. That recall button is used too much today. All it causes is more negative feelings towards someone who may not be totally at fault. Wouldn't you want someone, if they were angry at you, to be only focused on the present problem instead of years of frustrations.

Never forgetting is also a vicious mental cycle that leads to mental instability. There are many by-products of this type of attitude. Disappointments, bitterness, hate, and even murder. Yes, my friend, even murder. Most people murder in the heart first, before the physical act is carried out. It is imperative that we forget, or else we allow WHO to manifest those seeds to action. Are you ready to tie our impossibilities to line up with God's possibilities. Then meditate on God's word.

> Philippians 3:13-14: Brethren, I count not myself to have apprehended: but this one thing I do, forgetting those things which are behind, and reaching forth unto those things which are before, I press toward the mark for the prize of the high calling of God in Christ Jesus.

We decided to cover forgetting first, because we felt that our willingness to forget is much harder than our willingness to forgive. Most people know that we are to forgive, but didn't know until this point that we are to forget also. So, brother man, or sister woman, we need to ask for help in this area for it is impossible to do it alone.

> St. Matthew 6:14-15: For if ye forgive men their trespasses, your heavenly Father will also forgive you: But if ye forgive not men their trespasses, neither will your Father forgive your trespasses.

That's simply two of the easiest scriptures to understand! In most, if not all cases, even little children can grasp the meaning. However, if we are not taught the principle of forgiving, and we don't incorporate it into our daily lives, then it's no wonder there are so many failed past relationships. Forgiving should be one of those absolutes that is needed for our basic survival.

But, guess what—WHO definitely doesn't want us to forgive others. Not only will we carry around unnecessary guilt, but also a bag full of other negative emotions. These emotions will keep our minds so cluttered with junk, that it will almost be impossible to stay focused on life itself. We do need to smell the roses instead of smelling the garbage.

There are too many people walking around with a mind full of garbage. Their thoughts come out in their attitudes and interpersonal relationships with others. How can one have a nice day, when there is a world full of people like this?

Negative thoughts are always harmful to you and others. Some people wear their attitudes. You have seen some of the T-shirts. "I HAVE A BAD ATTITUDE." "SAME—DIFFERENT DAY." "PURE—." They either think like what they are wearing, or someone gave them the T-shirt, to show them how they really are. Whenever I encounter someone like that, I try to put as much distance between them and me.

To continue on this type of mental pathway, one can look forward to obstruct the present and destruct the future. Let's solidify that last statement. Remember disappointment, bitterness, hatred and murder. Those are sequences of thoughts. First, you are disappointed the affair did not go according to your plans. Secondly, you can become bitter, if the situation is not rectified according to your satisfaction. Thirdly, one starts to develop hatred towards that individual. And lastly, we will seek some type of justice in the form of revenge. Think about it for a moment, you may not have thought that way but, you either know or read of ones who have. Stop the sequence as soon as you see this pattern coming. If you have been guilty of it in the past, then forgive and forget.

Many states are passing stalking laws today. Many lives have been interrupted by revenge, motivated by failure. In some cases, people are afraid to meet new people without trying to secure some type of profile analysis. How can you blame them? There are a bunch of loony tunes walking around today. What if there had been this type of book around to help them, well that's why we know without a doubt that, this book is necessary now!!!

Listen to me, MR./MS. Reader—breakups are not suppose to end in hate or violence, but unfortunately some do. Some of you have no idea how much of an impact you would have on your X's or X,X,X,X's future by simply forgiving/forgetting out of a sincere heart. Your wellness is at stake. LET GO….FORGET AND FORGIVE NOW…

So is forgiving that simple? Yes, providing you are willing to let go of your PRIDE. Most often it's pride that tells you not to forget or forgive. Pride with a bad attitude is an immediate turn off. Having too high of a opinion of oneself. Hold on, before you crucify me—it's very healthy to have this type of opinion of oneself, providing that it lines up with the universal laws of mankind. There are limitations to this high opinion. When pride tells you that you are never wrong, and only what you think is important or right and you are constantly putting others down, then it's time to re-examine the true meaning of pride.

In the ME FIRST generation, selfish pride is of the foremost importance. The real problem occurs when you hook up with someone who thinks just like you. No one wants to give in first. Then you start keeping score on whose fault it is. Most of this is the mind game. Instead of treasuring the new found excitement of another person, to share life with, we play mind games on each other. "Somehow or some way I must come out on top," pride tells us. When pride is used as an offensive tool to ensure winning, then you, my friend, don't know how to lose. Losing or failures isn't always necessarily bad as I have said before.

> Psalm 119:71: It is good for me that I have been afflicted; that I might learn thy statues.

Learn from the past. The past can steer you away from present or future bad experiences. In order to see a clearer now, and in the future, you must apply the above principles. I know that I've learned to treat females with more respect and dignity. In turn, for the most part I get better treatment nowadays. Let go of the prideful past but, learn from it also.

> Psalm 51:10: Create in me a clean heart. O God; and renew a right spirit within me.

The next area we need to look at is our emotional state. If you are like most of us, our emotions have been severely damaged. Even when we try to apply the above principles, we are still hurting. So what is the answer? I really don't know your particular mental emotional state, but I know someone who does.

> Exodus 16:26: And said, If thou wilt diligently hearken to the voice of the Lord thy God, and wilt do that which is right in his sight, and wilt give ear to his commandments, and keep all his statues, I will put none of these diseases upon thee, which I have brought upon the Egyptians: for I am the Lord that healeth thee.

The emotional damage that occurred in my early teen years is now being dealt with as I write this book. The best thing that could have happened for me to receive my healing was to start to write this book. Never underestimate the power of THE ALMIGHTY GOD; the cleansing power of the LIVING WORD along with THE GREAT PHYSICIAN JESUS CHRIST aided by THE HOLY SPIRIT and his guidance.

Only recently did I realize how Christ cared for my emotional wellness. I had too much pride to really tell others how I was hurting or where the deep hurt was coming from. But I did turn to my friends for sympathy and consolation. I also turned to drugs and alcohol for mind changing and lots of sex for gratification which caused more problems than the ones I started out with. When I finally turned to Jesus, guess what—He was sitting there waiting for me. Jesus is also sitting there waiting for you!!!

Those unrecommendable outlets can, and will, kill you both physically and spiritually. Whenever you resort to drugs, alcohol, or sex outside of marriage for the relief of your problems, you don't realize how sick you have become or becoming.

When the mind gets to a state of dis-ease, and you try to ease it with indulgences, you will cause disease of the body, soul and spirit. One must be extremely careful what one stays focused on.

The hospitals, mental institutions, and doctor's offices are full of people who did not know how to guard their minds. You must come to a point in life, WHEN we must learn how to let go. On the other hand, you might think you can beat the odds. That would be very chancy considering the evidence that was just presented. So before you knock my viewpoints, be smart enough to try them. I know they work otherwise how can I be sitting here writing about them with the aid of my HELPERS.

Isaiah 26:3: Thou wilt keep him in perfect peace, whose mind is stayed on thee: because he trusteth in thee:

As difficult as the above steps are, how equally difficult is this step, but you have to incorporate this also for wellness and your willingness to let go. A point should be reached WHEN you realize the person you are trying to hold on to simply doesn't want you. That's an ego crusher if there ever was one.

You need to ask yourself some pointed questions and sincerely answer them to the best of your ability. No. 1—Why do you want them? No. 2—Do they really want you? No. 3—Are they available? No. 4—Do you have compatible lifestyles? No. 5—What are you willing to sacrifice to get them? No. 6—Have you asked God? Once you get through these series of questions, and you have formed some type of friendship or relationship with your dreamboat, then ask them the same questions and see what you come up with. Based on the answers, you should have a more clearer pathway to romance or a split-up. Wouldn't knowing help ease your mind?

Question #3 bears some additional comments. Are they available? Is this a triangle romance that you might be involved in? Everyone loses in a triangle. Even if you wind up one of the victors, you lose on the trust factor. Please don't let the involvement be with a married individual. Every dummy knows that doesn't work. WHO is constantly tricking people into this type of situation. WHEN you stay involved you cooperate with WHO. On the other hand WHEN you get out, or let go you are cooperating with God. It's always your choice. Do you know how many lives, and families have been destroyed by the triangle? Too many to even count. And unfortunately, many of us have been participants.

Look at the biblical account of a triangle affair. David—Bathsheba and Uriah. II Samuel 11, 12:1-24. Even today the media glorifies these type of affairs. They call it gossip, or news. You also need to try to determine whether or not this is passion or love. There is a difference. We have committed a whole section to this love question. Still it will boil down to your choice to hold or fold. Back to the dreamboat. Perhaps you need to ask one last question, that's if you are not sure yet. No. 7—How long am I going to wait? Gee I don't know. Another very pointed question. Maybe they will change, or maybe not. All I can tell you up to this date is I'm willing to wait on the Lord. However, I still have a life. I would rather wait on the Lord, than wind up with someone other than my queen. Everyone's circumstances are different. Plus in the past, I did the picking and choosing based on what I passionately wanted. Now I am at a point in life I would rather have what I need vs. what I want. The Lord knows my desire. My special lady has been ordered through prayer and faith. I had to apply the above principles because I was sure that a few ladies that I had met were the one. So you see, I also had to let go. The Lord had to change some of my ways of thinking and habits. Since most of us resist change, the process took longer than maybe it should have taken. Whenever I would get discouraged or impatient, I found comfort in GOD.

> Isaiah 40:31: But they that wait upon the lord shall renew their strength; they shall mount up with wings as eagles; they shall run, and not be weary; and they shall walk and not faint.

We could also let go of our lying. Maybe we should let that go NOW!! We often create these prefabricated tales about how much we don't need or want a mate. I find this so particularly prevalent in the body of Christ since I am also a member. This is true especially among some women, who sometimes try to fabricate how spiritual they are, instead of just being real. We all can find contentment in Christ Jesus, however, I was taught honesty is the best policy. This is by no means meant to be a verbal attack on our help meets, but start being real with yourself. Put into actions the above principles, and get a life. I had never met so many bitter women before in my life, until I got saved. God speaks about being unequally yoked. Therefore, we as the body of Christ, should be the example to this dying world. Have God-honoring, healthy friendships, that lead to relationships which should end in marriage.

Revelation 21:8: But the fearful, and unbelieving, and the abominable, and murderers, and whoremongers, and sorcerers, and idolaters, and all liars, shall have their part in the lake which burneth with fire and brimstone: which is the second death.

When you look at that particular passage of scripture, you just might see some of the negative things, habits, or ways of life we have tried to instruct you to forego. In conclusion, remember the aforementioned steps and put them into action. WHEN DO WE LET GO??? Unforgetting, unforgiveness, bad attitudes, pride, egos, triangles, the one?, and of course lying?; WE DO IT NOW THROUGH CHRIST JESUS. GOOD LUCK!

WHAT—IS THE PROBLEM??

Proverbs 18:24: A man that hath friends must show himself friendly: and there is a friend that sticketh closer than a brother.

Let's begin this section with a personal touch. It is May 21, 1992. It's 6:00 PM, Temperature is 75 degrees, and I am sitting on the West River Drive in Philadelphia PA. I am midway on this beautiful hill, alone on a blanket writing this section of this book. Fairmount Park, like most parks is simply beautiful at this time of the year. Flowers are in bloom, ducks are swimming in the Schuylkill River, while rowers are sculling in their boats. The pathways and roadways are full of joggers, bikers, runners and walkers.

Many people are cooking out in the open air, and there are three very beautiful females about fifty yards away. I just waved to them and they returned my gestor. At this point, I'm ready to put aside this project, and go join the ladies. If they would only invite me. This scene is picture perfect for companionship, but as I said before, I'm alone on this stupid blanket. Now as I further look around, I'm the only one here alone. Lord, wouldn't it be nice to have a friend to share this space and time.

Ask yourself this question, "How many times has this happened to you"; when all you wanted was friendship, there was no one there? That's why we need to move full speed ahead to find some answers to the proposed question. WHAT IS THE PROBLEM? Let's start to focus on what a friend is, or should be. We chose to use a format that centered around questions rather that a lot of opinions that could be called answers. However the word of God puts the proof in the pudding. Question No. 1—Do you know what a friend is? No. 2—Do you know how to make a friend? No. 3—Are you friendly to yourself and others? No. 4—Has the daily pressures of life stopped people from becoming true friends? No. 5—Has crime, violence, mistrusts, selfishness, diseases forced people into shells? The correct answers to these questions should be:

No. 1—yes, No. 2—yes, No. 3—yes, No. 4—no, and No. 5—no. WHAT did you come up with?

Unfortunately, there are too many people that have their yes's and no's in the wrong places. And that, my friend, is one of the problems. Hardly anybody is willing to start a friendship first, before starting a relationship. I for one, had no idea what a real or should I say, true, friend was. I always knew and interacted with lots of people, but I'm not sure that they were my true friends. Here are the initials of the exceptions. CJ, WJ, BM. I counted three, how many can you count?

> Proverbs 17:17: A friend loveth at all times, and a brother is born for adversity.

> St. John 15:13: Greater love hath no man than this, that a man lay down his life for his friends.

That's pretty heavy, but so should friendships be. Don't worry. Before Christ, my yes's and no's were screwed up also. Yes, Jesus Christ taught me the true meaning of friendship. If we did it God's way, we would have a ton of friends and one lifetime mate. Whenever I offend someone intentionally or unintentionally, The Holy Spirit will not let the offence go unchecked. My pride will either say I'm sorry, or ignore His prompting. My willingness to apologize created friends. It gave them opportunities to respond in kindness. You then leave each other on a positive vibe instead of on a negative. They just might want to interact with you again. This shows respect for their feelings, and they begin to like and want to be around you more often.

Earlier I mentioned The Golden Rule, and the application of that rule. If we were willing to follow that rule, we probably wouldn't need this book to be written. You might want to know how, for example, Jesus taught me about friendships. One easy answer would be for me to say, that He died on the cross. I'm not saying to go and lay down your life for your friends, because most of you would think that I was a little nuts. However, we need to be more sensitive to the feelings of others.

If, we could only get past the fear of rejection or non-acceptance, then friendships would be a lot easier to make. Making friends causes you to expose yourself to others. If you are not satisfied with the real you, then you should go to God and get a tune-up or overhaul. God runs specials every moment of our lives. He is ever present to teach if you want to be reached. Prayer out of a sincere heart is the simplest way for me. Then be willing to put into action 100% of what He tells you to do. God's words are his written guarantee. Won't you stop a moment and embrace this show of friendship and love displayed by Jesus?

St. John 1:11-12: He came unto his own, and his own received him not. But as many as received him, to them gave he power to become the sons of God, even to them that believed on his name:

Learn to take rejection, or non-acceptance in stride. The rejection still did not stop Jesus from dying on the cross. Form a healthy attitude so that when you are rejected, you might be given seed to a brighter horizon. There are close to five billion or more people on earth. Certainly you can find at least three friends like I did.

Sometimes, you just may have to be the one who will open up a new friendship. You just might have to use your smile muscles, or a pleasant greeting to help break the ice. Often, I have heard that a smile, like music, is a universal language. There is one thing that disturbs me a lot—all these sour faces walking around, who are forever asking me and others, "WHAT are you so happy about?" About life, you idiot, and the fact that I am alive and in a better state of wellness, than I ever have been before, and that's because of Jesus. Work on seeking to form a healthy, friendly attitude. Laugh a lot, get silly if you have to, but start to use those sixteen smile muscles vs. those sixty-four frown muscles.

Proverbs 15:13: A merry heart maketh a cheerful countenance: but by sorrow of the heart the spirit is broken.

Step No. 2—learn to love and appreciate you. Quit depending on someone else to help and ensure your happiness. By now, we should know that we telegraph our net self-worth by how we think, which comes out in WHAT we say about ourselves. We leave people no other choice but to say, "if he doesn't love, respect, and appreciate himself, then why should I." Now you have to understand the thin line between self-love and selfish love. Selfish love is a taker, rather than a giver. Both involved persons should be willing to expose both their strengths and weaknesses. They should be also willing to give 100%, 24-7.

As you give out, you allow room to receive back. Ideally the well will never run dry. You are very important and needful for a healthy friendship. We get too hung up on what we think others think about us. Man, whether you realized it or not they need and want friends too. We all have something to offer.

Basically, everyone is in the same boat. Put importance on what you have to share. Share you, with dignity, pride, respect, positive self image, motivated by love for others. YOU ARE SPECIAL!!

Psalm 139:14: I will praise thee; for I am fearfully and wonderfully made: marvelous are thy works; and that my soul knoweth right well.

Step No. 3—Be yourself from day 1. The real you will come out sooner or later. Don't start a relationship with deceit as its foundation. Nobody wants to be deceived or tricked into believing that you are something that you are not.

Often times, we would like to portray that we are so fun loving, kind hearted, sexy, charming, etc, etc, and etc. Even though we may have these capabilities, are they our dominant personality traits? Certainly, we have some things about us that we don't like. For me, I get moody at times and I need some space. When I take time to explain this unsociable type of characteristic, this will as least let people know what to expect when it is moody time. Then they won't have the security problem thinking that they have done something wrong, when in fact, it's me. That's only one of my WHAT'S. Moving right along.

It will be impossible to learn that much about each other in one or two meetings, but if you start the flow being yourself, you will find, or should I say, you ought to find a more relaxed atmosphere. Now don't go interrogating someone like you are the CIA or the FBI. Learn to be cool, calm and collective. Just be honest about yourself as the natural things flow. See, the things or response they might be looking for could possibly be how you really are and there you go blowing it by being deceitful.

Romans 12:17: Recompense to no man evil for evil. Provide things honest in the sight of all men.

On the other hand, if you see that you don't want to continue the friendship the way it's going, then be honest about that also. BE KIND BUT DON'T WASTE TIME. Ease the hook out, with compassion and understanding. You injure other people's emotions, by not doing this with care. Always remember, to do it with class. That person is also fearfully and wonderfully made by God.

We want to touch base with a biggie. This might not follow the above order. We need to know how to handle anger and stay friends. Bookstores are full of the how to. One suggestion is that you purchase one, or apply every aforementioned principles that's been given. It's that simple—this world has far too many angry and hateful people in it. The real big problem is that you and I have to deal with these timebombs. Who needs, or wants, a timebomb? Shortfused individuals are a menace to those who desire peace in relationships. When I run across women like that, I try to steer them to the word of God A.S.A.P.

Ephesians 4:26-32: Be ye angry, and sin not: let not the sun go down upon your wrath: Neither give place to the devil. Let him that stole steal no more: but rather let him labor, working with his hands the things which is good, that he may have to give to him that needeth. Let no corrupt communication proceed out of your mouth, but that which is good to the use of edifying, that it may minister grace unto the hearers. And grieve not the Holy Spirit of God whereby ye are sealed unto the day of redemption. Let all bitterness, and wrath, and anger, and clamor, and evil speaking, be put away from you, with all malice: And be ye kind one to another, tenderhearted, forgiving one another, even as God for Christ's sake hath forgiven you.

STOP THE WAR!!! What war, you might be asking? The ongoing war between the sexes. Ever since the Garden of Eden, you know WHO has been working his mess. Aren't you getting tired of his foolishness? He seems to be intensifying it even more today. Since I know there is nothing new under the sun, this warfare is simply getting more air time. We ought to be thankful, that we think, and act differently from each other. We should appreciate our gender uniqueness. The fact is that from first glance we should be able to tell male from female. My rule of thumb is, if I have trouble at the first glance, then I assume that there is a problem somewhere.

II Timothy 4:7: I have fought a good fight, I have finished my course, I have kept the faith:

In today's Hi-Tech, live and in color, ever changing world, WHO has turned up the warfare between the sexes. It is now very unpopular and demeaning for some to say, "that men and women have roles in which they should operate in." There is a segment in today's society that refers to motherhood as something very base. On the other hand, if you are a father, you should be making all this money to have any worth in society. I came from two hard working parents, who work together, who also taught me to work with my mate. My foremost problem was one of a fidelity nature rather than understanding what role I was playing today. My parents did together, what needed to be done. They stayed together until the Lord took my mother.

Ephesians 4:3: Endeavoring to keep the unity of the Spirit in bond and peace.

Have you ever wondered why WHO didn't tempt Adam and Eve together. Perhaps he might not have been so successful. Hummm—now think about that for awhile. Obviously, you should be seeing a more clearer picture by now of his devices. He causes division. Then once he does that, he conquers, or destroys your relationship. He caused the Gap and he is causing a lot of your problems. We are too busy blaming, and fighting with each other to mount an attack against the real enemy. Since we have established that there is warfare being fought, then we should start to prepare to fight to win this war together. Join forces through prayer as soon as possible especially with newer friendships. This also works on very old ones too.

> Ephesians 6:10-18: Finally, my brethren, be strong in the Lord, and in the power of his might. Put on the whole armor of God, that ye may be able to stand against the wiles of the devil. For we wrestle not against flesh and blood, but against principalities, against powers, against rulers of the darkness of this world, against spiritual wickedness in high places. Wherefore take unto you the whole armor of God, that ye may be able to withstand in the evil day, and having done all, to stand. Stand therefore, having your lions girt about with truth, and having on the breastplate of righteousness; And your feet shod with the preparation of the gospel of peace; Above all, taking the shield of faith, wherewith ye shall be able to quench all the fiery darts of the wicked. And take the helmet of salvation, and the sword of the Spirit, which is the word of God: Praying always with all prayer and supplication in the Spirit, and watching thereunto with perseverance and supplication for all saints;

Most of us, have had to hustle, scratch, scrape, and fight for everything we have gotten worthwhile. One of the last things that I want to do is fight with my lady. I'm not necessarily speaking of the physical aspect of fighting. Mental warfare is as devastating as the physical. If we could see the scars of mental warfare, we would be surprised. We need to stop this foolishness. When WHO can divide, he can and will conquer. Don't get mad when WHO does his job, you get even. Band together to work your friendships out. Destruction is one thing that WHO is very good at. He's had a lot of practice at it. But we can defeat him and his devices through Jesus Christ.

Well, we have covered some basic problems that have plagued some of my past relationships. Obviously, there has to be many more. Otherwise there would be more lasting ways people relate to each other. I'm trying to end this section, but in my spirit, there seems to be more we should talk about.

This, I feel, should have been included in the WHEN—DO WE LET GO section under compatibility, or incompatibility. And that is, how to, and I am putting this as softly as I can, get rid of the NUTS. I have been extremely fortunate in a lot of ways. So far, I have not had the misfortune of having a relationship with a NUT. Some people are mentally unbalanced when you meet them. You just might have been, or will be, the prey that they are looking for. That's a huge problem, and I mean huge!!

Some people thrive on abuse. They love confrontations, whether physical, mental, or experimental. Since I haven't had to experience this type of situation, my first hand knowledge is limited.

However, down through the years, I have had some friends, or associates, that were involved in some. All that I can remember, was that they went through _ell. At one stage in my life, I abused women trying to be a man. Abuse nearly cost me my life, never again will I do something as stupid as abuse. To clear things up, my physical abuse never got past a slap or push, but that was wrong, almost dead wrong. Now I see why I couldn't stop where I wanted to. See, yes, in the past, I was a jerk too.

One thing I did learn from the experiences, was that: No. 1—as smart, and as right, that I thought I was, I still couldn't out talk a woman. Which of course infuriated me. Conclusion to No. 1: men, don't hit, and women, don't push a man too far. No. 2: when you resort to any kind of abuse, you have a self-esteem problem. Most often, you are looking for anything to trigger this emotional disturbance. So in reality, it's not the situation, it's you. Conclusion to No. 2 admit that you need help, and get it right away.

> II Corinthians 10:3-6: For though we walk in the flesh, we do not war after the flesh: (For the weapons of our warfare are not carnal, but mighty through God to the pulling down of strongholds;) Casting down imaginations, and every high thing that exalteth itself against the knowledge of God, and bringing into captivity every thought to the obedience of Christ; A having in a readiness to revenge all disobedience, when your obedience is fulfilled.

The two popular movies, that typifies the type of NUTS that I first spoke of are "PLAY MISTY FOR ME" and "FATAL ATTRACTION". I have no plan of action for people who get involved with people like that. But there is one thing that I can say. You best seek divine help before you get started. That's why we need to seek the omniscience of ALMIGHTY GOD. God is all knowing and he will certainly steer us away, if we are willing to obey.

> Psalm 34:14: Depart from evil, and do good; seek peace and pursue it.

Now, I think we are ready for a new chapter. My only hope is that you are not getting too bored with THIS, GOD WILL YOU HELP ME WITH THIS

BOOK? Now if, you have friends or have need of friends, focus on these areas, and start to make applications for the world's sake and yours: No. 1—Learn and earn friendships. No. 2—Love, respect, and appreciate yourself and others. No. 3—Be yourself and be honest about you, and be truthful to others. No. 4—Learn to handle anger, and know what to properly do about your anger. No. 5—Stop the war NOW. Band together in love, respect, and dignity. No. 6—Seek God's guidance first. Look before you leap. If you meet a NUT, give them a copy of this book.

> Proverbs 3:5-6: Trust in the Lord with all thine heart; and lean not unto thine own understanding. In all thy ways acknowledge him, and he shall direct thy paths.

DO WE REALLY KNOW—WHAT LOVE IS????

What's your answer to this intriguing question? We all may have opinions, but not necessarily concrete answers. On the other hand, there may be some people who have solved this highly controversial question. My answer is quite frankly NO, but I think I'm getting closer to an answer that would help me to learn how to love. If someone would have asked me that some years back, I would have told them YES. But now I see, that my knowledge, was basically limited to feelings that existed for the moment. I love to be loved. That is man's basic need, however it is more to love than that. There are many types of love that will be covered. But I don't want to do them now. I'm chomping at the bit to go into another direction now.

Love was to me, and is somewhat, an expression of one's feelings towards others. Most often, it was usually how they would express their feelings towards me first. I had the old, me first, No. 1 selfish attitude towards love. The what's in it for me, if you can get my drift. Also I, felt that true love was based solely on feelings and emotions.

I learned to somewhat control my feelings and emotions for defensive purposes. Every now and then I would run into someone who thought like me, and of course that never worked out, because no one was willing to give love, only to receive it. Also to be very honest, once the thrill was gone, so was I. No wonder I'm reaping those seeds that I once sown. We must pay somewhere down the line, when we selfishly misuse others.

Love is not all passion. But lots of people think that's what it is. If you have a dynamite, passionate love affair with your married mate, then you know you have something special. Outside of marriage all you have is SIN!

Enough of that. In the preceding section on WHEN, many people stay in crazy, sinful situations because of passion, did you know that? Passion can be a disguise called love. People will say these three words, with no idea of what they are saying, or the effect it has on others. I LOVE YOU. Once, I found out that some ladies actually believed me, I quit that part of my sin. LYING. Since we commonly align love with sex, we can readily see, we have two problems here: No. 1, we don't know what love really is, and No. 2, a sin problem, lust and lies.

St. John 8:44; Ye are of your father the devil, and the lust of your father ye will do. He was a murderer from the beginning, and abode not in the truth, because there is no truth in him. When he speaketh a lie, he speaketh of his own: for he is a liar, and the father of it.

Now, the Lord just told me, that you're getting upset with me. All I need to do is tell you this, the enemy wants you to stay confused so that he can continue to tell you believable lies. If you remember how we opened, and that was "know the truth and the truth shall make you free"—you have just experienced one of his cunning and crafty devices, and that is, the denial of the truth. We had to tell you that now. That statement is a statement of authority, because God is God. Can't you now see the emotional damage of those dual sins? No wonder there are so many messed up people, who tried it WHO's way.

Another one of my wild thoughts concerning love was, THE IDEAL. I simply focused on appearances, positions, vocations, financial statements, social ties, family backgrounds and etc., etc., and etc. I better stop before you get really steamed, Those qualifiers are extremely important, providing they are placed in proper order.

Esther 2:17: And the king loved Esther above all the women, and she obtained grace and favor in his sight more than all the virgins; so that he set the royal crown upon her head, and made her queen instead of Vashti.

This was usually my sequence of thought. First by getting with them, they would evaluate my financial, social, and or economic status. There again, there's nothing wrong in hoping and dreaming. You better believe this as fact. I for one, wanted to marry a very rich woman for the identical same reasons, and would do it today, if she's the one. However we must be equal on grounds of compatibility of what we can both offer each other, spiritually and physically, our true motives and understanding of the union of marriage, and the blessings from the LORD. I hope that I didn't leave anything out of my desires for a mate. Money and fame does not ensure happiness, but they can get you things and recognition. What you have to decide is, can things, and places fulfill the need to love and be loved.

III John 2: Beloved I wish above all things that thou mayest prosper and be in health, even as thy soul prospereth.

From that statement of fact, it looks like God has always wanted me to have the best. What I need to do is stay lined up with His word and be willing to do it his way. Then, without a doubt I will have what God knows I need and can handle. I don't ever remember having a No. 2 reason. Therefore we need to go on.

> Isaiah 65:24: And it shall come to pass, that before they call, I will answer; and while they are yet speaking, I will hear.

Since you and I can not change the past, let's see if we can do something about our now and future. One thing I have learned that Love is not lust, deceit, personal gain, or fleshly desires. Maybe if I can continue to eliminate what I once thought, then perhaps I can come up with the real answer. In some cases, we must give up something to get something. I think I know what I want. The problem is, that I don't know what to give up. Therefore I'm left with no other choice but to pray.

> "My heavenly Father, I come to you now in faith believing that you will answer me. First, I give you all the praises, glory and honor. I come to your throne of grace to worship you. I give you sincere thanksgiving of praise for all you have done for me. I pray for the wisdom to write this book and the pathway in which you are leading. For my eternal hope is to be in your presence throughout all eternity. I come to you with reverence and humility. Only because of Jesus Christ, your Son and my Savior, who is sitting at your right hand interceding for me in my behalf. If I have done anything displeasing in your sight, I ask your forgiveness. If my thoughts have not been right, or if I have unforgiveness in my heart also forgive me. Whatever unrepentant deeds that I have done against you and others, I humbly ask forgiveness. I thank you for your mercy and grace that you have allowed me to live, and have provided so many blessings which are too numerable to mention. All I can say out of an sincere heart is thank you. Thank you for this urging to come to you now to receive my deliverance from the past sown seeds. I only ask, that those of whom I selfishly touched, that they will also forgive and forget. That from this day forward, I accept your forgiveness and forgive myself, and will not let the devil condemn me anymore about the past. My request is that you show me the areas in which you want, and know that I need to let you have. That I will continue to grow in your grace and love so that I can share it with others. That you will strengthen me with might by your Spirit in the inner man. To do your will and to surrender my will so that you can and will continue the work you have started. I also pray for this

world, that your kingdom come and that your will be done on earth. I pray for every need for humanity sake. I pray that we as a nation will turn back to you before it's too late. Have mercy on us. We are your highest form of creation. Just show me, and give me the spirit of obedience to surrender all to you. I thank you for The Holy Spirit you have left to comfort, guide, correct, and instruct me so that my actions might be pleasing to you. I thank you for our talk. And for the ear to hear when you answer. The determination to apply your word to my life. I ask and thank you in Jesus Christ my Savior's name. Amen."

> I Corinthians 13:4-7: Charity suffereth long, and is kind; charity envieth not; charity vaunteth not itself, is not puffed up, doth not behave itself unseemly, seeketh not her own, is not easily provoked, thinketh no evil; rejoiceth not in iniquity, but rejoiceth in truth; bearest all things, believeth all things, hopeth all things, and endureth all things.

I Corinthians 13, is commonly known, throughout most of Christendom as, The LOVE Chapter. We have been taught, that the word "charity" is also translated into the word "love" from the original Greek language. So when you read this again, substitute, the word charity for love, to see if your definition of love lines up with what God is saying. Like I said before, my initial answer was YES, I know the meaning of love. Did my actions line up with it's meaning? If the walk doesn't line up with the talk, then all you have is words. And that's WORD!!

Are you ready for the most profound statement, that I would like to say that I coined. "ALL ACTIONS PRECEED THOUGHTS." Yes, good buddy, you think first then you act. It doesn't matter how fast you act or have acted. It's your thoughts and thought process. We need to learn to re-direct our thoughts. I certainly had to, or else someone else could or would be possibly writing this book. It's a fact, God wants this book published to help his children. However, if not me then someone else. I said earlier that it was a blessed privilege to yield to HIM for this project's completion.

Now back to those verses. People have stated that the Bible is its own interpreter. Therefore I don't intend to interpret these verses for you. My only hope and intent, is that we can point out to you some very interesting facts or opinions. Secondly, that what we point out, will be beneficial for understanding and application. Thirdly, how love relates to you and, how you relate to love and it's model meaning.

CHARITY SUFFERETH LONG: It takes time and patience for this area to manifest itself into your being. By exercising patience with yourself and others seems to be most helpful to gain understanding. I don't think anyone has determined the amount of time this process takes. Adjustments in getting to know someone new, and then learning to peaceably co-exist with them is paramount. Would it be fair to say, that the length of time that you are willing to allow, could possibly measure the amount of love you have for that individual. God waited 35 years for me to say YES to Him. But God IS God and we are mere humans. Plus God's love is everlasting. We, as stated before, have a tendency to bring the past with us into our present. Then we say, "here I am, now love me". Most often we have some unpleasant attitudes, and some not so good behavioral problems. We are sometimes not sure whether we even love ourselves. The picture is not always that bleak. We also bring happiness, wellness, joy, and high self-esteem and many more positive personal attributes. A lot of relationships started out on solid foundations and are successful and thriving.

On the other hand, how long are you willing to wait for things to balance out? We can wait, but sometimes it takes divine help to accomplish this desired goal. One should begin to show and maintain a willingness to change and re-adjust our thought process for love's sake. Start to view and review ourselves as God and others see us. Build on the positive character traits, and by all means possible, get rid of the negatives. Let the Holy Spirit, Word of God, or whatever methods deemed necessary change you. But change we must. This is your first building block.

AND IS KIND: Have you taken time today to be kind to someone? Kindness takes on the flavor or attitude of doing something pleasant to or for someone. Usually, when the act of kindness is being performed, one would gain some type of joy and happiness. Brother, just by being kind to some people is all they need to make it through the day. That's how important love with kindness means to us humans. When kindness is done from a sincere heart, man, they can't help but love you. When you find someone that doesn't respect or appreciate the act of kindness, then my friend, it's time to move on, and move quickly!!

A certain lady who I would like to get to know much better is dating someone else. She is aware of my feelings, but she doesn't ignore me, or make me feel indifferent. All I can say is Praise The Lord. I really admire the way she has handled this situation, and I am led to get her a nice friendship card just to tell her that. I have gained quite a bit of respect for her. She had a choice to be kind or unkind.

CHARITY ENVIETH NOT: We really don't need to write that much about envy. We all know that envy and jealousy are cousins. Both are sins, and have caused many discomforts in life for us and others. Those three words are very self-explanatory. Am I correct? So if envy is in our hearts, then get it out before it destroys you and others.

Proverbs 27:4: Wrath is cruel, and anger is outrageous; but who can stand before envy.

CHARITY VAUNTETH NOT ITSELF, IS NOT PUFFED UP: "I don't and won't always be first in everything." This piece of the love puzzle goes against the normal way. As you hang in there, you can clearly see how the steps of growth to love takes time. Putting others first places self second or third at times. This growth process requires a lot of right thinking before spontaneous actions. As you live out this component of love, no one should have to ask you if you love them or not. They will know, because of your actions that defeats pride arrogance and selfishness.

DOTH NOT BEHAVE ITSELF UNSEEMLY: Since good is the opposite of evil, then love should be the opposite of hate. Good and love go hand in hand, while evil and hate are a like. Man's natural sinful nature usually leans towards the latter, therefore it seems that we have to be taught to do good and to love. People are forever looking at what we do, as well as what we say. It behooves us to practice what we preach, for credibility sakes and our wellness. Think and do what is right. Quit being the bad egg. Once we know what to do, then love does it regardless of our feelings.

SEEKETH NOT HER OWN: This area will show you, who the real you is. Who is really first and foremost. You or your mate. Have you ever wondered why there are so many T.V.s in our modern day homes? We need them to keep peace in the homes because everyone has a favorite show that they like. It's a tough choice when they basically come on at the same time. Sports vs. talkshows, sitcoms vs. drama, variety shows vs. educational shows are but a few examples in which this type of love will be put through the test. This portion of love will share and give in without getting mad, angry or furious when it doesn't get its way. This type of love will sit down and watch it with you and learn to gain enjoyment, because they are with the one they love. Now don't go and throw all your T.V.s away, but certainly you will start to see and realize whose on first.

IS NOT EASILY PROVOKED; A short fused person is a menace to this world's society. You never know when they are ready to explode about nothing. When you mix this with self-centeredness, you have got big problems. That's pretty clear cut. We need to find where one's sensitive areas are, and stay away, from, or off them. However, as we see how our behavior affects others, we need to stop and think sometimes to realize what we're doing.

As you are being developed in this area, using the T.V. scenario, this love doesn't get too up tight when asked to watch football, or be ignored for the next six months. This is the real taking portion, and it definitely hurts most of the time. So tell your partner to ease up—for you have feelings too.

THINKETH NO EVIL: Remember when I stated that actions preceeds thoughts? You think and then act. Then, if that's true, and it is, then there should not be any excuse when we offend each other. Most often we mean to do it. We often insincerely apologize for this is the proper thing to do. It didn't just happen, you thought to do it. Wisdom is knowing what to do and then doing it.

> Proverbs 23:7: For as he thinketh in his heart, so is he: Eat and drink smith he to thee, but his heart is not with thee.

REJOICETH NOT IN INIQUITY BUT REJOICETH IN TRUTH. BEAREST ALL THINGS, BELIEVETH ALL THINGS, HOPETH ALL THINGS, ENDURETH ALL THINGS, CHARITY NEVER FAILETH.

You have been given a barometer from God to go by. That's God's Agape Love for us to use as a guideline to live by and interact with. Yes, it's possible to start the achievement process. Since God has given this to us, then it only makes sense to me to ask Him to help us put this into action for our lives. There are other types of love which also must be incorporated into our lives. Such as brotherly, sensual, or love for siblings. However, the same principles apply. You can't get around them. So now I ask again the question. DO YOU REALLY KNOW—WHAT LOVE IS? May the blessings of the Lord reward you richly in your endeavor to find the right answer from the right source. Look, I'm seeking and learning myself and I can emphatically say I'm blessed to be on the right road.

> Proverbs 10:22: The blessing of the Lord, it maketh rich, and he addeth no sorrow with it.

HOW—DO WE
RE-CONSTRUCT OUR
LIVES???

All truth has foundation. When you have something that needs repairing, you should get THE INSTRUCTION MANUAL, and/or RETURN IT TO THE MANUFACTURER. Since that theory applies to most of the products we have purchased, then why don't we return ourselves to our maker?

> Genesis 1:26-27: And God said, Let us make man in our image, after our likeness: and let them have dominion over the fish of the sea, and over the fowl of the air, and over the cattle, and over the earth, and over every creeping thing that creepeth upon the earth. So God created man in his own image, in the image of God created he him; male and female created he them.

My all wise and all everything HELPERS are the creators of all mankind. That's why we must be returned to the creator for an overhaul, and for re-construction. Once we realize that truth and understand its logic, then our common sense should tell us that's the proper thing to do. When you purchased a toaster, for instance, it usually comes with a guarantee, a warranty, instructions, and product return information. Now man is smart enough to realize that the product might give us some problems at a later date. That's why God has given us a manual for instruction called the BIBLE. Within its pages, you will find the necessary tools for reconstruction. All the how to's are contained within these sixty-six books.

> Psalm 139:14-17: I will praise thee; for I am fearfully and wonderfully made: marvelous are thy works; and that my soul knoweth right well. My substance was not hid from thee when I was made in secret, and curiously wrought in the lowest parts of the earth. Thine eyes did see my substance, yet being unperfect; and in thy book all my members are written, which in continuance

were fashioned, when as yet there was none of them. How precious also are thy thoughts unto to me, O God! How great is the sum of them!

We did not evolve from monkeys. But if you want to believe the evolutionary theory, then I strongly suggest that you visit your local zoo, and visit the primates section, to see if monkeys aren't having little monkey babies. Also see if they have any people manuals of instruction as to how to live etc., etc. and etc. Just a little of my sarcasm to keep you interested.

St. John 3:7: Marvel not that I said unto thee, Ye must be born again.

You really need to read for your self the entire Book of Saint John. Yes, it's that simple. Just like the toaster—we malfunction at times. We need lots of love and a good overhaul or renewing of the mind. There are a lot of broken hearts out there that need mending. Many lives are in such a mess, it's no wonder why we act the way we do at times. Once we realize the need for new birth, you will be well down the road of wellness.

The aforementioned healing principles contained in the previous chapters are the keys you need to unlock the door to happiness. They usually go against the normal way of thinking, but dare to be different. When we have been hurt, the usual reaction is to hurt back. God and His word tells us to love back. See, that's the difference. Most people expect us to get even in some way or another. The new birth gives you the comfort and consolation ministry of the Holy Spirit. Had it not been for the new birth, I would be still holding the hurts, pains, and unforgiveness in my heart today. I need to tell you that my physical and mental health has improved drastically, for I am more AT-EASE now. Remember when I earlier stated that DIS-EASE causes disease of the mind and body (they call it stress today).

The new birth is spiritual. God is a spirit. When the Holy Spirit resides on the inside, and Jesus Christ intercedes in our behalf—boy, we've got the things we need to affect lives rather than infect lives. We need that new solid foundation to help attain love, joy, peace, and happiness. By the way, that's what you want, don't you?? BEING BORN AGAIN, will rid your mind of junk, bitterness, and the heartaches of the past. So if you're not by now, get what I've got. YE MUST BE BORN AGAIN!!

St. John 14:6: Jesus smith unto him, I am the way, the truth, and the life: no man cometh unto the Father, but by me.

The libraries and bookstores are full of books on this subject. I won't comment or criticize another man's work until I have read them. I stated earlier that I hadn't completed any research on this matter prior to the start of this project. I still maintain that fact. However, my THREE HELPERS should be given the glory, and their teachings embraced. I would not have gotten this far without their help. Only Christ can give you the accurate knowledge you need. We have been deceived too long by WHO and worldly wisdom. Most people will agree that this planet is in bad shape. Ask the average baby boomer. Things are getting increasingly worst. We all can point back to a time or event that has taken place in our lives as well as society, and say that's when we started having our problems. That's why you can depend upon Jesus to help you. Jesus proved his everlasting love at the cross.

Prayerfully, go back to the manufacturer. Ask him to fix the parts and give you a new heart. God is always there willing to listen to whatever is on your heart and mind. Jesus functions now as our High Priest, our intercessor, a Wonderful Counselor, and He is The Prince Of Peace. What else do you need? But you must go to him. He's waiting.

> St. Matthew 11:28-30: Come unto me, all ye that labor and are heavy laden, and I will give you rest. Take my yoke upon you, and learn of me; for I am meek and lowly in heart: and ye shall fine rest unto your souls. For my yoke is easy, and my burden is light.

Growth always necessitates change. That's fact No. 4, I think. Who cares what number we are on anyway? Change we must, if we are to grow. I just said that only in a different way. We are the sum total of our thoughts. Our thoughts produce actions, and our actions indicate our character and the way we handle life's pleasures and pressures. No one can handle the exact situation the same way each time. Therefore, we have the capabilities to change whenever we desire to. It can be positive or negative depending on our thought process. You have to decide to change to infect or affect.

This present day's society and its bending towards immorality has caused severe damage to our youth and some weak minded adults. I know from experience how easy it is to be influenced in a negative way in order to gain acceptance from peers. A true leader will follow the truth and do the right thing regardless of the crowd. Unfortunately, there aren't many true leaders willing to take a stand for righteousness. But you can and so can I. Let's for a moment look at some attitudes that I was confronted with as a late teen and young adult. "One night stands," "Do your own thing," "Rebellion of the sixties," "The freedom of a new drug culture," just to name a few. WHO said you're grown and you can do whatever you want to do? That's not the way my friend. Yes, I knew better, because my parents spent years training me, only to let them and myself down. It's not worth trying it your way.

> Proverbs 22:6, 23:13-14: Train up a child in the way he should go: and when he is old, he will not depart from it. Withhold not correction from the child: for if thou beatest him with a rod he shall not die. Thou shalt beat him with the rod and shalt deliver his soul from hell.

One statement that's off my original topic. I know that all the child's rights groups will be at my throat, but that's what God is saying and I agree with God. Had it not been for my foundation in righteousness, I would not have had a clear option to determine unrighteousness.

> Colossians 2:8: Beware lest any man spoil you through philosophy and vain deceit, after the traditions of men, after the rudiments of the world, and not after Christ.

The Virgin Mary who gave birth to our Lord and Savior was chosen because, yes, you got it, she was a virgin. Mary made a quality decision to follow God's commandment. Look at the results of being obedient to God. My daughter Brandi is sixteen years old. She has promised me that she will remain a virgin until she goes to college. My prayer and instruction to her is to remain a virgin until she gets married. The greatest gift a woman can give to her husband is her virginity.

Men, you are definitely not off the hook either. Save yourself for marriage. Most of the people who will read this book have failed God, themselves, and their future mate in this area. Don't worry you are only one sincere prayer away from obtaining a clean slate with God.

By nature we want items that are new. Most men talk the talk of desiring a virgin, and I, also fitted in that same category. The only problem was, I don't remember us saying that we wanted to marry her first. Our thought process was out of proper order. Think for growth.

> Philippians 4:8: Finally, brethren, whatsoever things are true, whatsoever things are honest, whatsoever things are just, whatsoever things are pure,

whatsoever things are lovely, whatsoever things are of good report; if there be any virtue, and there be any praise, think on these things.

See, I told you, reconstruction required spiritual and mental change for growth. God is certainly able to facilitate your change when you make up your mind. You must discipline yourself to avoid those deadly traps. Yes, you know what traps. Most of us has set a few ourselves, only to be snared by them. At some point in our lives, we must reap what we have sown. That's a natural law as well as a spiritual law that operates whether we believe it or not. We used to say "what goes around comes around." Same meaning. I know I have been in the reaping season, for quite some time, and I definitely don't like what I once sown. How about you? Even though I am under God's love, grace, and mercy, still the law must be applied to my life also. I didn't realize how much I had planted and how sick I had been all those years. But thanks be to God who gives us the victory. The next fundamental truth is that we will be used by God, Satan, others, or your own flesh. We all would like to think that we act as independents. However, that's not always true. Something or someone motivates our action. Ponder on that for a moment or two.

The fact is we follow principles, guidelines, natural and spiritual laws, motives, and suggestions. There are right and wrong ways of thoughts, actions, or deeds on any given subject matter.

I Corinthians 6:12: All things are lawful unto me, but all things are not expedient: all things are lawful for me, but I will not be brought under the power of any.

God's does not take all the fun out of life as some people suspect. He has set up laws and commandments that we should obey for our own good, and the betterment of all mankind. Look for a moment at the drug culture. It was cool when you or I abused our bodies with them. Look at the escalation and what it is doing to our society today. That's one minute example. Apply it to any of your enjoyable acts of disobedience to God's laws and you should see a more clearer picture. God is omniscience and has all the right solutions to help us in the discipline area. Yes, our problem solver is Jesus and the ministry of the Holy Spirit. They are omnipotent, omniscience, and omnipresent. They will and want to help us reconstruct our lives.

St. John 14:16, 26, 16:7-13: And I will pray the Father, and he shall give you another Comforter, that he may abide with you for ever; But the Comforter, which is the Holy Ghost, whom the Father will send in my name, he shall teach you all things, and bring all things to your remembrance, whatsoever I have said to unto you. Nevertheless I tell you truth; It is expedient for you that I go away: for if I go not away, the Comforter will not come unto you; but if I depart, I will send him unto to you. And when he is come, he will reprove the world of sin, and of righteousness, and of judgement: Of sin, because they believe not on me; Of righteousness, because I go to my Father, and ye see me no more; Of judgement, because the prince of this world is judged. I have yet many things to say unto you, but ye cannot bear them now. Howbeit when he, the Spirit of truth, is come, he will guide you into all truth: for he shall not speak of himself; but whatsoever he shall hear, that shall he speak: and he will show you things to come.

That's only part of the helping hand Christ left for us. As you get to know the Holy Spirit and his ministerial responsibilities, it will literally blow your mind. Thank you Jesus for my help which cometh from the Lord. I don't know if you noticed in verse 14:16, when Jesus called the Spirit, the Comforter.

I for one didn't embrace that part of his ministry until recently. When in pain most people want comfort, am I correct? Well, you got him there for you. The Holy Spirit will also instruct, lead, correct, and chastise you when you need it. If you want and are willing to obey his instructions, you will become the person you were created to be. Our problem is, we don't want anybody telling us what to do. God or otherwise. Well, good buddy, that's called rebellion. I was one of the most rebellious people I have ever known and still have in me now, but as they say, "you can't beat city hall." Pray with and for me as I continue to surrender that part of my will, and bring it under the authority of the Holy Spirit. I will be praying for you.

Proverbs 3:11-12: My son, despise not the chastening of the Lord; neither be weary of his correction: for whom the Lord loveth he corrected; even as a father the son in whom he delighteth.

Now I know where my parents got that from when I was being chastened, and they would say that this hurts me more than it is hurting you. Well, thank you, Mommy and Daddy. You did it because I needed it, and because you loved me. One area that the Holy Spirit is dealing with me is late night T.V. No, not the sex channels. But some programs are a little more revealing than others, and that's usually the time, outside of pro sports, that I watch T.V. It gets too hot in the kitchen so I need to stay out. Get my drift? Late night T.V. isn't bad, but it's too lustful for a single man who is trying to keep his flesh under the control of the

Holy Spirit. His instructions was to "turn the T.V. off and go to bed." If I want victory, I will obey. If not, then do I truly want reconstruction?

> Romans 6:13: Neither yield ye your members as instruments of unrighteousness unto sin: but yield yourselves unto God, as those that are alive from the dead, and your members as instruments of righteousness unto God.

Don't let something as simple as turning off a stupid T.V. cause you to commit a stupid sin!! DISCIPLINE YOURSELF. God has given us His power. All you have to do is use it. You must start to take control of your life and your weak areas. Life really isn't that complicated IF you are willing to yield ye your members.

So as not to bore you, we can't cover every little issue. But when you APPLY the suggested principles that line up with the word of God, you will be RECONSTRUCTED. God will even send you all the help you need. Don't get down on yourself if you stumble and fall at times. Just be determined to walk. You have seen little babies when they attempt to take their first steps. I have messed up more than a few times myself during my reconstruction stage. By the way, if you haven't guessed yet, that's where I am and will probably stay until Jesus comes back for me. This particular section is where most of us are anyway. RECONSTRUCTION is never ending. We all have a long, long, very long way to go until we think we have it right. Be open and ready to obey THE HELPERS. Victory is mine and yours. God would not have it any other way.

> Romans 7:15-25: For that which I do I allow not: for what I would, that do I not; but what I hate, that do I. If then I do that which I would not, I consent unto the law that it is good. Now then it is no more I that do it, but sin that dwelleth in me. For I know that in me (that is, in my flesh,) dwelleth no good thing: for to will is present with me; but how to perform that which is good I find not. For the good that I would I do not: but the evil which I would not, that I do. Now if I do that I would not, it is no more I that do it, but sin that dwelleth in me. I find then a law, that, when I would de good, evil is present with me. For I delight in the law of God after the inward man: But I see another law in my members, warring against the law of my mind, and bringing me into captivity to the law of sin which is in my members. O wretched man that I am: who shall deliver me from the body of death? I thank God through Jesus Christ our Lord. So then with the mind I myself serve the law of God; but with the flesh the law of sin.

That's why you'd best stay in a constant reconstruction type attitude. We, at this point, feel you have been given enough information to get started, and enough reasons to remain in the Creator's care. This section has truly been a blessing to write.

I thought because I had made some progress in some areas, I was cool; but The Holy Spirit just informed me how badly I needed to stay in RECON-STRUCTION. So hang in there. By the way, I LOVE YOU!!!

I am very sorry for telling you that I had finished this section. When I reviewed my second re-write, I noticed that we had written the steps we need to aid in our reconstruction process. So please bear with me. I guess I was a little too anxious to go the next section entitled, WHERE—IS MY MATE? Thanks for your patience. Listed below are some principle steps for reconstruction. We decided to utilize a checklist type approach, and a work page to help you develop a workable system for you.

APPLICATIONS

1. RETURN TO MAKER
2. USE INSTRUCTION MANUAL—THE BIBLE
3. BE BORN AGAIN—YOU'RE SPECIAL
4. JESUS IS THE WAY
5. PRAY FOR HELP
6. CHANGE FOR GROWTH
7. DISCIPLINE TO STAY
8. DEVELOP RIGHTEOUS THOUGHT PROCESSES
9. OBEY GOD'S WORD AND HOLY SPIRIT
10. APPLY ABOVE STEPS FOR RECONSTRUCTION

A famous shoe company uses three little words to help market their shoes. They simply say "JUST DO IT." That's it. It's that simple. Use the whole court—GOD THE FATHER, GOD THE SON, and GOD THE HOLY SPIRIT.

> Psalm 119:105-112: Thy word is a lamp unto my feet, and a light unto my path. I have sworn, and I will perform it, that I will keep thy righteous judgements. I am afflicted very much: quicken me, O Lord, according unto thy word. Accept, I beseech thee, the freewill offerings of my mouth, O Lord, and teach me thy judgements. My soul is continually in my hand: yet do I not forget thy law. The wicked have laid a snare for me: yet I erred not from thy precepts. Thy testimonies have I taken as a heritage for ever: for they are the rejoicing of my heart. I have inclined mine heart to perform thy statues always, even unto the end.

WHERE—IS MY MATE??

I don't know, for I am still looking for mine. Just a little humor to start us off. But in reality, I don't know. But you and I can rest assuredly, that there is someone out there for us. We also must consider the ratio of available men to available women. So from jump street, you might have figured out, that this section would be the most difficult to write. Because if I could come up with that type of information, I would be more than wealthy in a very short time.

There are, and have been, quite a few services that try to match and mate. A lot of them have been very successful in putting folks together. We are very confident, that by putting the principles into actions that you have read so far, that you will also find your correct mate. The one that's a perfect fit. One term you might hear me say from time to time is "MY PRIME RIB"—that's the one I desire from the Lord. Prime ribs have always been my most ordered beef when I dine out. Particularly a well prepared end cut.

> Proverbs 18:22: Whoso findeth a wife findeth a good thing, and obtaineth favor of the Lord.

So, my friend, I am going to seek the Lord, and hopefully wait on Him for an answer. My reason for responding that way is, I have looked long and hard and still no results. I had two very good choices early in life and blew them, causing pain and problems in our lives. God had to do some house cleaning, some repair work, and probably finish this book before he could TRUST ME with another person's life. God's a lot smarter than me. He knew I wasn't ready. I didn't realize it until we really got into this book. He promises to supply our NEED. Obviously, I didn't need a wife then. However, I was especially desirous of one during my moments of lonesomeness. It took a while, however. The Holy Spirit has given me much comfort during those bad times of complaining. Now I am more sensitive and sensible to accept God's sovereignty.

Believe me, I, like you have made persistent pleadings to him, but wait we must. There is absolutely nothing wrong with constantly bathing your request with prayer. We should pray until we get an answer from God. Why would God command us to pray if he could or didn't intend to answer our prayers? Yes, before I go on, "To pray is to obey." You sin when you won't, or don't pray. Did you know you can give God your specific desire concerning a mate?? One problem is that you might not know what you really need, since God supplies our NEED. Take some time to really think, then ask him. Be detailed enough to write down what you really desire in a mate. Everything from head to toe. Please include the character traits, temperament, compatibilities, educational, and the rest of the etc.'s, etc.'s and etc.'s. Be completely specific with God. Also tell him the areas that you feel you are unable to compromise with at this point in your life. Since your order might not necessarily be filled by tomorrow, review and revise if necessary. Usually when you see that you need to change your initial description, you just might find out that you have grown in some area. And that my friend deserves a big PRAISE THE LORD.

PRAISE OF A VIRTUOUS WOMAN

Proverbs 31:10-31: Who can find a virtuous woman? For her price is far above rubies. The heart of her husband doth safely trust in her, so that he shall have no need of spoil. She will do him good and not evil all the days of her life. She seeketh wool and flax, and worketh willingly with her hands. She is like the merchants ships; she bringeth her food from afar. She riseth also while it is yet night, and meat to her household, and a portion to her maidens. She considereth a field, and buyeth it: with the fruit of her hands she planteth a vineyard. She girdeth her loins with strength, and strenghteneth her arms. She preceiveth that her merchandise is good: her candle goeth not out by night. She layeth her hands to the spindle and her hands hold the distaff. She stretcheth out her hand to the poor; yea, she reacheth forth her hands to the needy. She is not afraid of the snow for her household: for all her household are clothed with scarlet. She maketh herself coverings of tapestry; her clothing is silk and purple. Her husband is known in the gates, when he sitteth among the elders of the land. She maketh fine linen and selleth it; and delivereth girdles unto the merchant. Strength and honor are her clothing; and she shall rejoice in time to come. She openeth her mouth with wisdom; and in her tongue is the law of kindness. She looketh well to the ways of her household, and eateth not the bread of idleness. Her children arise up and call her blessed; her husband also, and he praiseth her. Many daughters have done virtuously, but thou excellest them all. Favor is deceitful, and beauty is vain: but a woman that feareth the Lord, she shall be praised. Give her of the fruit of her hands; and let her own works praise her in the gates.

One thing you should try to understand is the sovereignty of God. God does what He wants, when He wants to, and how He wants to do it. That's the waiting and growth and development part of reconstruction. There are millions of people who understand that fact, but find difficulty in the patience area. Also, we have to factor in the conditions that have to be met in order for our prayers to be answered. There are over 800 promises recorded in the Bible. Most all of us know what a promise is. Well, then you can rest assured, that God has kept, and is able to keep, whatever He says.

> Numbers 23:19: God is not a man, that he should lie; neither the son of man, that he should repent: hath he said, and shall he not do it? Or hath he spoken, and shall he not make it good?

> I Kings 8:56: Blessed be the Lord, that hath given rest unto his people Israel, according to all that he promised: there hath not failed one word of all his good promise, which he promised by the hand of Moses his servant.

So the next real big question that needs to be dealt with is, "what are the conditions, and/or requirements that God expects from us for Him to answer our prayers and keep His promises?" To find out that answer, it would be silly for me to give you my opinion. Looks like the smart thing to do would be to ask God. So here is his answer.

> Deuteronomy 10:12-11:1: And now, Israel, what doth the Lord thy God require of thee, but to fear the Lord thy God, to walk in all his ways, and to love him, and to serve the Lord thy God with all thy heart and with thy soul, to keep the commandments of the Lord, and his statutes, which I command thee this day for thy good? Behold the heaven and the heaven of heavens is the Lord's thy God, the earth also, with all that therein is. Only the Lord had a delight in thy fathers to love them, and he chose their seed after them, even you above all people as it is this day. Circumcise therefore the foreskin of your heart, and be no more stiffnecked. For the Lord your God is God of gods, and Lord of lords, a great God, a mighty and a terrible, which regardeth not persons, nor taketh reward: He doth execute the judgement of the fatherless and widow, and loveth the strangers in giving him food and raiment. Love ye therefore the stranger: for ye were strangers in the land of Egypt. Thou shalt fear the Lord thy God; him shalt thou serve, and him shalt thou cleave, and swear by his name. He is thy praise, and he is thy God, that hath done for thee these great and terrible things, which thine eyes have seen. Thy fathers went down into Egypt with threescore and ten persons; and now the Lord thy God hath made thee as the stars of heaven for multitude. Therefore thou shalt love

the Lord thy God, and keep his charge, and his statutes, and his judgments, and his commandments, always.

The summation of the whole thing is that God wants and requires OUR LOVE, OUR REVERENTIAL FEAR OF GOD, AND OUR OBEDIENCE ALWAYS. Now isn't that what most, if not all parents want from their children? God is not any different. We have to give it to Him. If you have formed the good habit of love and obedience to God, don't you think you could start to channel that same type of attitude toward someone whom you also love?

Wouldn't it be beautiful to be caught in a cycle of love, instead of the vicious cycle of lust and lies? The minute you start to enjoy your reconstruction, you will find yourself on the road to your mate. God's the potter and I am the clay. Do you intend to succeed? Then expect a miracle. You are that miracle. Think of the joy that Jesus provides for all of those who are His. My basic instincts relates to, and picks up on joyful people. I love to be around those types. You might want to start being more joyful in spite of the conditions that surrounds us daily. Start today by being a blessing to others. GO OUT OF YOUR WAY TO BE PLEAS-ANT. It does not matter if that person does not respond in kind. Remember you are planting new seeds of love, joy, and kindness that will by all means manifest themselves. Remember to tell the Lord that you love him also.

People have asked me, "why do I want to remarry?" That's very simple. I intend to do it God's way. I don't like failing. You may have realized by now, that the righteous way is the only way to go. With all these marriages failing today, why would anyone want to do it? The answer is that they might not be going at it the right way. Your mate also might be very apprehensive about tying the knot.

That's where your patience and understanding will come into play. Therefore take this free time to discuss everything you want, likes or dislikes, desires, wants, and needs that you expect from a marriage and a mate. Be so truthful that you are willing to leave no holds barred. If you see that it's a match, then still proceed with caution. If it's not a match, then be loving, kind and courteous and move on, but leave with the friendship in tact.

I know that I have a lot to offer, and so do you. That's why you should expect a miracle. You should, with all the determination you've got, do whatever is nec-essary to offer the best you to the right mate. I know some of you are not willing to give that much of you at first. But remember most of us want that type of giv-ing to be given to us. Somebody's got to start first, why not you? We have learned what God requires, and have written down what we desire. Now we are really on our way to meeting Mr./Ms. RIGHT. Share these precious moments we have on earth with joy and high expectations. Cooperate with God to find a PRIME RIB or be that found PRIME RIB.

> I Thessalonians 4:3-4: For this is the will of God, even your sanctification; that ye should abstain from fornication: That every one of you should know how to possess his vessel in sanctification and honor;

What you have just read is God's general will for our lives. And when you back that up with His word in Genesis where He says:

> Genesis 2:18: And the Lord God said, It is not good that man should be alone; I will make him a help meet for him.

You can clearly see what God's design for our lives is. Once I read that and the Holy Spirit illuminated it to me, I no longer will doubt God. Now I know I can't demand anything from Him, but that does not stop me from expecting the best from God. Our hope and sincere prayer is that we elevate our standard of living that it agrees with God's requirements of holiness.

Holiness is very unpopular in our immoral society. But it can and will be done. Too many people are caught between two opinions. God's ways vs. the world's ways. God insures love, joy, peace, grace, mercy, and life. The world promotes lust, lies, pleasure, sin, sickness and death. But only you can make that decision. Will you make the right choice to find your PRIME RIB, or are you the findable PRIME RIB?

> James 1:5-8: But let him ask in faith, nothing wavering. For he that wavereth is like a wave of the sea driven with the wind and tossed. For let not that man think that he shall receive anything of the Lord. A double-minded man is unstable in all his ways.

What if, as you finished the last page of this book, he/she is also finishing their last page? And you both decide to put these principles into action right away, and met and lived happily ever after? That possibility can and will happen for someone. I was led to place that here now. Miracles can happen. Consider this what if. What if you don't and you miss out on your miracle. Who will you blame this time? I know this will work. Not because I said it, but because God is saying it.

You must consider that you are about to bring another person into your life. God is no respecter of persons, he loves them equally as he loves you. Be willing to do the responsible requirements that are needful for a God honoring relationship. If you are not willing to do it God's way, then leave it alone. If you're satisfied being single, you have nothing to be ashamed about. My one suggestion is that you also, if you have not already, get a purpose and meaning in and for your life. The big price we must pay is that we have to give. Give up of self in order that two become one.

So, Mr. Writer, you still haven't told me WHERE my mate is? Are they hidden away in some secluded spot? I still don't know!! Maybe I don't know the exact location, but this I do know:

> Psalm 24:1: The earth is the Lord, and the fullness thereof; the world, and they that dwell therein.

O.K., what is the meaning? Be ready, or stay in a state of expectation that you might meet them at any time or place. It may be the person who just placed a ticket on your illegally parked car. Now you know how you would feel towards a person who did that, don't you? The point I'm making, is that you don't know who they are. We need to be more mindful of how we treat one another. You never know. You have heard the old expression that "first impressions are lasting impressions." Also "what have you done for me lately" is quite popular also. Try all that's in you to treat everyone according to the "GOLDEN RULE." Seize back the control of your mind by thinking good, and better things will happen for and to you. Just go out and enjoy life with expectations of miracles.

Attitudes affect altitudes in everyone's life. Attract vs. repel. You can catch more bees with honey than with vinegar. All these little catchy phrases have enormous meaning concerning the new you. You may need to venture out a little further. Go home or shop at a different store. Break some of those normal ways and places you go. Be open and very sensitive to the leading of the Holy Spirit. You might even have to say hello back, when someone speaks to you. You definitely will have to ask God's divine guidance. LEARN TO BE FRIENDLY AND MAKE NEW FRIENDS. Don't always go places with the same group. Break the normal rut that you are in. Learn to be the new you. Visit a different church or church's group activity. All of this is in God's earth, so seek his counsel for directions.

REMEMBER God grants new mercies and grace each day. It is our responsibility to treat each person with respect and dignity. You don't know who you will meet throughout the course of the day, and how they are divinely placed in your life.

EVERYBODY you know, knows somebody. If you exhibit the character traits that a friend they know might require, they just might introduce you to them. How we meet, treat, and maintain the new persons that are allowed to come into our lives, can determine the level of our successes.

Don't try to seek and keep a mate by using your flesh. Stay in primary reconstruction as long as need be. LET THE BEAUTY OF SALVATION RADIATE LOVE OUT OF A SINCERE AND PURE HEART TO OTHERS. Honor and show compassion to all along life's journey.

Well it's been, like I said, a privilege to allow MY HELPERS' thoughts to flow in and out of my mind in order to share with you some basic truths about—WHY SINGLE—. Today's date is June 26, 1993. I truly thank GOD for my first book. I praise his name for giving me the necessary tools that were needful for its completion. So now we have come to the end and ready for copyright. GOD BLESS YOU and we close with GOD'S love and conclusion:

I WOULD LIKE TO LEAVE YOU WITH THIS LAST STATEMENT: GOD COMMANDS MEN, "TO LOVE YOUR WIVES." GOD FURTHER COMMANDS WOMEN "TO SUBMIT TO YOUR OWN HUSBAND." APPARENTLY, HE FOREKNEW THAT THIS WOULD BE A PROBLEM AREA FOR US. MY ADVICE IS TO APPLY THAT ALSO TO YOUR SINGLE LIFE AND SEE WHAT HAPPENS.

> Ecclesiastes 12:13-14: Let us hear the conclusion of the whole matter: Fear God, and keep his commandments; for this is the whole duty of man. For God shall bring every work into judgment, with every secret thing, whether it be good or evil.

THE END

0-595-31091-5